Pandora 的箱

Pandora's Box

retold by Henriette Barkow

illustrated by Diana Mayo

Chinese translation by Sylvia Denham

mantra

很久，很久以前，在盤古初開時，活著一群神和女神。

萬神之王 Zeus 坐在奧林匹克山上，覺得世界是美麗的，只是
缺少了某些東西，他仔細看清楚後便斷定世界需要動物、雀鳥
和魚。

Long long ago, at the beginning of time, lived gods and goddesses.

　　Zeus, the king of the gods, sat on Mount Olympus and thought that the
earth was beautiful but also that something was missing. He looked closer
and decided what was needed on earth were animals and birds and fishes.

Zeus 召了兩名泰坦巨人來見他，他們是 Prometheus 和
Epimetheus，Zeus 吩咐他們執行任務，製造所有動物，讓他們
在世上居住。「這裡有一個袋，裏面有一些特別禮品，你們用
來送給你們的作品吧。」他告訴他們說。

Zeus called the two Titans, Prometheus and Epimetheus, to him and
gave them the task of creating all the creatures to live on the earth.
"Here is a bag with some special gifts that you can give to your creations,"
he told them.

Prometheus 和 Epimetheus 兩兄弟就像很多兄弟一樣，各人有自己的長處和弱點，Prometheus 的名字有深謀遠慮的意思，亦是兩兄弟中比較聰明的一個，正如他的名字，他經常可以預見未來，亦因爲這樣，他警戒 Epimetheus 說：「我不會時常在這裡，你要好好保管 Zeus 的禮品。」

Prometheus and Epimetheus were brothers, and like many brothers each had his own strengths and weaknesses. Prometheus, whose name means forethought, was by far the cleverer, and as his name suggests, he could often see into the future. Thus it was that he warned Epimetheus: "I won't always be here, so take great care with any gift that Zeus may give."

雖然 Epimetheus 不及他的兄長般聰明，但他擅長製造東西，就好像一個雕刻家或木匠一樣，他製造各式各樣他想像出的動物，然後將 Zeus 的各種禮品分別送給他們，有些得到長頸，有些則獲贈斑紋和尾巴，尖嘴及羽毛。

Although Epimetheus wasn't as clever as his brother, he was good at making things, like a sculptor or a carpenter. He created all the creatures that he could think of and gave them different gifts from Zeus' bag. Some he gave long necks, others he gave stripes and tails, beaks and feathers.

當他造完後，他將所有動物展示給 Prometheus 看，「你認爲怎
樣呢？」他問他的兄弟。

「他們實在神奇，」Prometheus 說。

Prometheus 環觀世界，跟著想到另一種動物 — 一種以神爲模
式的動物。他取了一些泥，加一些水，然後造出第一個人。

跟著他爲這個人造了一些朋友，令他不會孤獨。

When he had made all the creatures he showed them to Prometheus.
"What do you think?" he asked his brother.

"They are truly wonderful," said Prometheus.

Looking across the earth Prometheus then had the idea for another
kind of creature - one that would be modelled on the gods. He took
some clay and added some water and moulded the first man.

Then he made him some friends so that man wouldn't be lonely.

當他造完後，他讓 Zeus 看他的作品，Zeus 便將生命吹送到這些人的身上去。

When he had finished he showed his creations to Zeus who breathed life into them.

Prometheus 和 Epimetheus 教人怎樣照顧自己，他倆留在世上教人怎樣去狩獵，怎樣建造庇護居所和種植食物。

有一天，Prometheus 到 Zeus 的袋子去拿禮品給他的作品時，卻發現袋子是空的，長鼻子給了大象，長尾巴給了猿猴，最大的吼叫聲送了給獅子，飛翔給了雀鳥，一樣一樣的送出了，直至再沒有任何其他禮品。

Prometheus and Epimetheus taught man how to look after himself. They stayed on earth and lived with man teaching him how to hunt, build shelters and grow food.

One day Prometheus went to Zeus' bag to find a gift for his creations but the bag was empty. The trunk had been given to the elephant, the long tail had been given to the monkey, the biggest roar to the lion, flight to the birds and so it went until there were no more gifts.

Prometheus 越來越喜愛他所製造的人，想送一些特別的禮品給
人，讓他們有較舒適安逸的生活，他看著他的作品，於是想出
一個念頭－火，他會將火送給人。
但是火是屬於萬神的，Prometheus 只能靠偷取才能將火送給人。
Prometheus 在黑暗中爬上奧林匹克山，盜取細少的火燄送給人，
他教導人怎樣令火繼續燃燒，以及火的各種用途。

Prometheus, who had grown very fond of his creations, wanted something special to give to man, something that would make his life easier. And as he watched his creation the idea came to him — fire. He would give man fire.

Now fire belonged to the gods and the only way that Prometheus could give fire to man was by stealing it.

Under the cloak of darkness Prometheus climbed Mount Olympus and stole a tiny flame and gave it to man. He taught him how to keep the flame alive and all that man could do with fire.

Zeus 不久便發覺人類有一些不屬於他們的東西，一些屬於萬神的東西，但神是不能將一些送了出去的東西取回的，Zeus 很惱怒，在憤怒之際，Zeus 決定懲罰 Prometheus 和人類。
Zeus 抓著 Prometheus，用鐵鏈將他鎖在懸崖上，那種痛楚簡直是難以忍受，但這還不夠，Zeus 要 Prometheus 受更多苦。

It didn't take long for Zeus to see that man had something that didn't belong to him, something that belonged to the gods and a gift given by a god could not be taken back. Zeus was furious and with all the rage and wrath of a god he decided to punish both Prometheus and man.

Zeus grabbed Prometheus and chained him to a cliff. The pain was almost unbearable but that wasn't enough for Zeus, he wanted Prometheus to suffer even more.

Zeus 於是叫神鷹撕裂 Prometheus 的肝臟。每一晚，Prometheus
的肝臟會愈合，但到天明時神鷹會回來，再啄食折磨
Prometheus。
這是沒有止境的痛楚，因此 Prometheus 便注定永遠受苦，沒有
任何希望。

So Zeus sent an eagle to tear out Prometheus' liver. Every night his
liver would heal and every morning the eagle would return, to torment
and torture Prometheus even more.

This was pain without ending, and thus Prometheus was doomed to
suffer forever without hope.

懲罰完 Prometheus 後，Zeus 考慮怎樣向人類報復，他想出一個狡猾的計謀，一個只有神才想得出來的計策。他製造另一個人，樣貌皓似一個女神。

他製造了一個女人，並將生命吹送到她的身上去。

Having punished Prometheus, Zeus devised a cunning plan to take his revenge on man. A plan that was worthy of a god. He created a being that looked like a goddess but was a human.

He created woman and breathed life into her.

Zeus 呼召所有其他的神和女神到來，吩咐他們各自將一份禮物送給這個女人。Aphrodite 送美麗給她，Athena 送出智慧，Hermes 送她精明的舌頭，而 Apollo 則將音樂送給她。Zeus 將她定名為 Pandora，然後送她往世上居住。

Zeus called the other gods and goddesses to his side and asked them each to give woman a gift. Among the many attributes, Aphrodite gave woman beauty, Athena gave her wisdom, Hermes gave her a clever tongue and Apollo gave her the gift of music.
Zeus named her Pandora and sent her to live on earth.

一個由上天創造，並擁有萬神所賜的各樣禮物的女人
實在是無法能抗拒的，Epimetheus 愛上了 Pandora。
在他們結婚的那天，Zeus 將一個很漂亮和玄妙的箱子
送給他們。
「享用這份禮物可愛之處，好好保管它，但切記，切
記，永遠都不能打開這個箱。」
可憐的 Pandora，在眾多神所賞賜的禮物中，Zeus 亦加
入了好奇心。

A woman made in heaven, with the gifts of the gods, was impossible to resist
and Epimetheus fell in love with Pandora.

On their wedding day Zeus gave them a beautiful and intriguing box.
"Enjoy the beauty of this gift, and guard it well. But remember this
- this box must never be opened."

Poor Pandora, Zeus had woven her fate, for amongst the
gifts of the gods was the gift of curiosity.

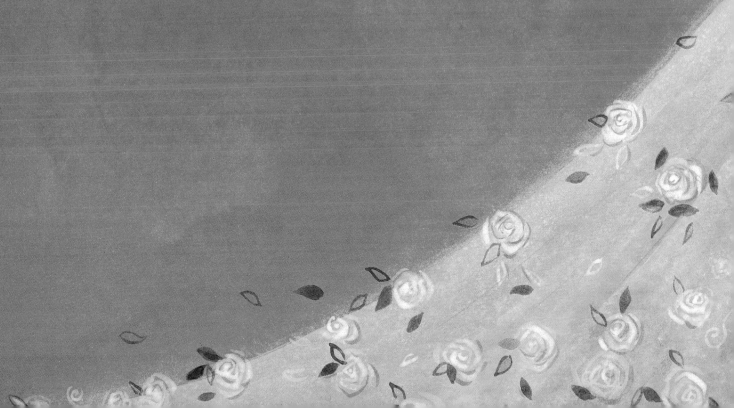

Pandora 和 Epimetheus 起初生活得很快樂，世界亦是一個富裕及和平的地方，沒有戰爭，沒有疾病，沒有哀傷，也沒有苦難。
當 Epimetheus 日間出外工作時，Pandora 精明地運用她的好奇心，尋找新的食物烹調方法，以及彈奏新音樂，她研究周圍的動物和昆蟲，向人類指示使用火去烹煮食物和製造金屬的新方法。

At first Pandora and Epimetheus were very happy. The world was a rich and peaceful place. There were no wars or illnesses, no sadness or suffering.

While Epimetheus was out all day Pandora used her gift of curiosity wisely. She found new ways to prepare their food and new music to play. She studied the animals and insects around her. Pandora showed man new ways of using fire to cook and work metals.

但好奇心是兩邊倒，同時有好壞兩方面的影響的。雖然 Pandora 做了很多好事，但她始終不能忘記那個封閉著的箱，每一日她都會去看它一看，每一日她都記得 Zeus 的話語：「永遠都不能打開這個箱！」

But curiosity is a double-edged sword, and for all the good that Pandora had done she could not put the locked box out of her mind. Every day she would just go and have a look at it. And every day she remembered Zeus' words: "This box must never be opened!"

過了幾個月，Pandora 又坐在這個箱前，「我只偷偷看一下裏面不會有問題吧？」她問自己道，「裏面不至於有甚麼那麼可怕的啊？」她周圍看一看，確定沒有其他人，於是從頭髮中拔出髮簪，仔細地撬開箱鎖。

　　After some months had passed Pandora found herself sitting in front of the box again. "What harm would it do if I just sneaked a look inside?" she asked herself. "After all what could possibly be in there that is so terrible?" She looked around to make sure that she was alone and then she took a pin from her hair and carefully picked the lock.

一旦箱鎖被撬開後，箱蓋反彈，箱子迅
即打開。箱內所藏著的可怕東西和被解
禁到世上的苦難實在難以用字句來形容。

As soon as the lock opened, the lid flew back and the box
burst open. It is hard to explain in words the terrible things
that were stored within that box and the suffering that
was unleashed upon the world.

當箱蓋打開時，憎惡及貪心、瘟疫及疾病、以及所有今日依然折磨世人的可怕事物皆飛躍出來。

When the lid was lifted, out flew hate and greed, pestilence and disease and all the terrible things that still torment us today.

當 Pandora 看到後，她震驚得立即抓住箱蓋，用盡全力將它蓋上。
她筋疲力盡地坐在地上哭泣。
「讓我出來呀！讓我出來呀！」一個細小溫柔的聲音叫道。
Pandora 擡頭去看這甜美的聲音從何而來。

Pandora was so shocked when she saw what she had done, that she
grabbed the lid and forced it down again with all her strength.
Exhausted she sat on the ground and sobbed.
"Let me out! Let me out!" cried a small and gentle voice.
Pandora looked up to see where this sweet voice was coming from.

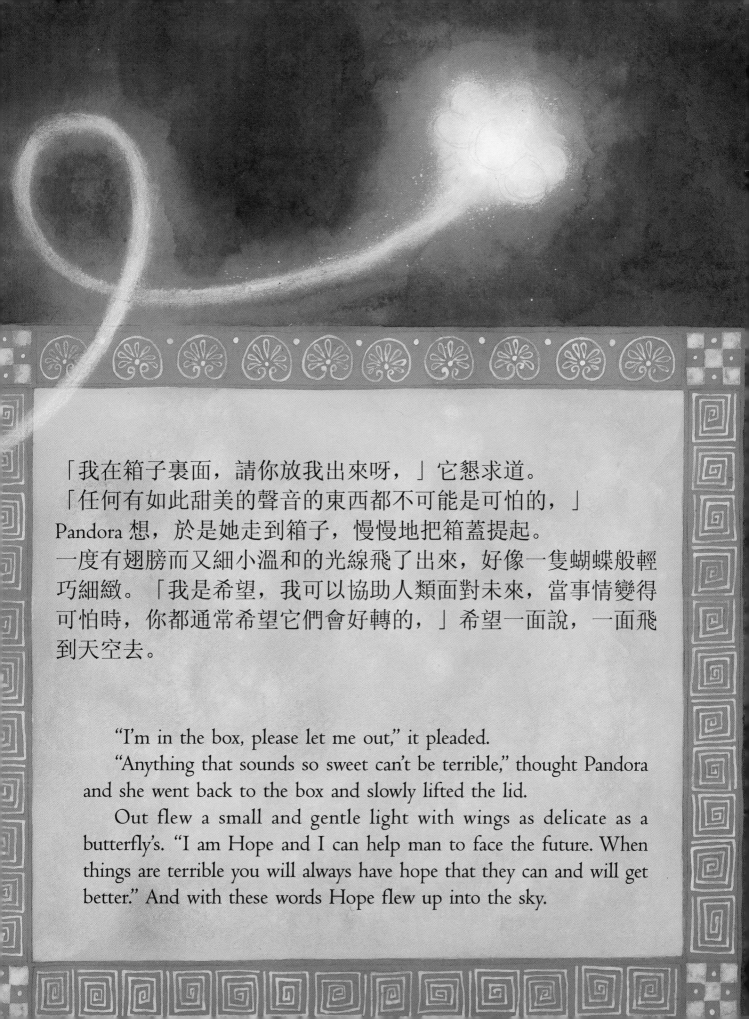

「我在箱子裏面，請你放我出來呀，」它懇求道。
「任何有如此甜美的聲音的東西都不可能是可怕的，」
Pandora 想，於是她走到箱子，慢慢地把箱蓋提起。
一度有翅膀而又細小溫和的光線飛了出來，好像一隻蝴蝶般輕巧細緻。「我是希望，我可以協助人類面對未來，當事情變得可怕時，你都通常希望它們會好轉的，」希望一面說，一面飛到天空去。

"I'm in the box, please let me out," it pleaded.

"Anything that sounds so sweet can't be terrible," thought Pandora and she went back to the box and slowly lifted the lid.

Out flew a small and gentle light with wings as delicate as a butterfly's. "I am Hope and I can help man to face the future. When things are terrible you will always have hope that they can and will get better." And with these words Hope flew up into the sky.

當希望遊歷世界時，它經過被困鎖在山上的 Prometheus，並觸摸他的心肝。

Prometheus 要多等幾千年，才會被 Hercules 釋放，但正如他們所說，那又是另一個故事了。

As Hope journeyed across the earth it passed Prometheus chained to the mountain and touched his heart.

It would take a few more thousand years before Heracles set him free but that, as they say, is another story.